Overcoming Witchcraft

by
Rick Joyner

MorningStar Publications

A DIVISION OF MORNINGSTAR FELLOWSHIP CHURCH
P.O. Box 440
Wilkesboro, NC 28697

Overcoming Witchcraft

Table of Contents

Part I

The Stronghold of Witchcraft

The practice of witchcraft has dramatically increased throughout the world in recent years. One of the expressed goals of this movement is to destroy biblical Christianity. Many Christians are presently suffering some form of attack from those who practice witchcraft. Discerning the nature of these attacks, and knowing how to overcome them, is becoming crucial for all believers.

We are exhorted not to be ignorant of the enemy's schemes (see II Corinthians 2:11). Peter warned us, **"Be of sober spirit, be on the alert. Your adversary, the devil, prowls about like a roaring lion, seeking someone to devour. But resist him, firm in your faith" (I Peter 5:8-9).** Understanding Satan's schemes significantly increases our advantage in the battle. The entire church age has been one of spiritual warfare, which is increasing as we approach the end of the age. Those who refuse to acknowledge the reality of this warfare and fight against it are being quickly overcome.

Satan is now being cast out of the heavenlies and down to the earth, where he is coming with great wrath. Even so, we need not fear—He who is in us is much greater than he who is in the world (see I John 4:4). He who is least in the kingdom of God has more power than any antichrist. But just as the greatest military power today is vulnerable if it does not recognize the enemy's attack, we, too, are vulnerable if we do not recognize Satan's schemes. The only way that he can defeat us is through our own ignorance or complacency. As we maintain our position in Christ, taking on the full armor of God and remaining vigilant, we will not only stand, but will prevail against the gates of hell.

What Is Witchcraft?

Witchcraft is counterfeit spiritual authority; it is using a spirit other than the Holy Spirit to dominate, manipulate, or control others.

In Galatians 5:20, the apostle Paul named witchcraft or **"sorcery"** as one of the deeds of the flesh. Though witchcraft has *its origin in the carnal nature of man*, it usually degenerates quickly into demonic power. When we try to use emotional pressure to manipulate others, it is a basic form of witchcraft. When we use hype or soul power to enlist service, even for the work of God, it is witchcraft. When businessmen scheme to find pressure points while pursuing a deal, this, too, can be witchcraft. Many of the manipulative tactics promoted as sales techniques in marketing are basic forms of witchcraft. The primary defense against counterfeit spiritual authority is to walk in true spiritual authority. Establishing our lives on truth and trusting in the Lord to accomplish what concerns us are essential keys to becoming free from the influence and pressure of witchcraft.

It is written that Jesus is seated upon the throne of David. This is of course a metaphor, for Jesus does not sit upon the literal throne on which David sat. But David established a position of true spiritual authority that would ultimately be manifested in the kingdom of God. David did for spiritual authority what Abraham did for faith. How did David establish a seat of true authority? Basically, he refused to take authority or seek influence for himself, but completely trusted in God to establish him in the position that He had ordained for him. David did not lift his own hand to seek recognition or influence, and neither must we if we are going to walk in true spiritual authority rather than mere human political power.

Any authority or influence that we gain by our own manipulation or self-promotion will be a stumbling block to us and will hinder our ability to receive true authority from God. If we are going to walk in true spiritual authority, like David, we will have to utterly trust in the Lord to establish us in it in His time. As Peter exhorted, **"Humble yourselves,**

therefore, under the mighty hand of God, *that He may exalt you at the proper time"* **(I Peter 5:6).**

Einstein once made an observation that may be more important than his theory of relativity, though it is utterly simple. He declared that, "Premature responsibility breeds superficiality." There is possibly nothing more devastating to our calling and potential for walking in true ministry than seeking influence or authority prematurely.

When the Lord promotes, He also supplies the grace and wisdom to carry the authority. There is no greater security available than knowing that God is the One who has established our ministry. Few things can breed insecurity faster than trying to maintain a position that we have gained by our own promotion or manipulation. This is the root of most of the territorial preservation and division that exists in the body of Christ.

Being established in true spiritual authority is a fortress that simply cannot be penetrated by the enemy. Paul explained that **"the God of peace will soon crush Satan under your feet" (Romans 16:20).** When we know that we have been established by God, we have a peace that utterly crushes the enemy.

In contrast, when we establish ourselves in a position of authority we have little peace; the more our illegally gained influence increases, the more striving and manipulating it will take to hold it together. Anything we do through manipulation, hype, or soul power, regardless of seemingly noble goals, is doomed to ultimate failure.

Therefore, the first principle in being delivered from the influence of witchcraft is to repent of all the ways that we ourselves have used it in our own lives and ministries. Satan cannot cast out Satan. Witchcraft, in even its most evil and diabolical forms such as black magic, will have an open door into our lives if we ourselves are using manipulation for controlling others or gaining a position. Although we may try to justify using such devices in order to build the church, God is not fooled and neither is the enemy. What God is building is not raised up by might nor by power, but by His Spirit. Whatever we build by any other means is an affront to the cross and will ultimately oppose that which the Spirit is doing. The flesh wars against the Spirit, regardless of how good we try to make the flesh look.

Using the Gift of Discernment

Discernment of spirits is a primary gift of the Holy Spirit that enables us to distinguish the spiritual source of influences in the church. However, much of what is considered "discernment" today is really *"suspicion,"* rooted more in fear and self-preservation than in the Holy Spirit. This is because so much of the authority that is exercised in the church today is counterfeit, which causes those who use it to be striving, fearful, and intimidated by anyone that they cannot control.

True spiritual discernment is rooted in love.

Love is patient...kind...not jealous... does not brag, and is not arrogant,

does not act unbecomingly; it does not seek its own, is not provoked, does not take into account a wrong suffered,

does not rejoice in unrighteousness, but rejoices with the truth;

bears all things, believes all things, hopes all things, endures all things (I Corinthians 13:4-7).

Although we may be concerned that the readiness to bear, believe, hope, and endure all things will lead to naivete rather than to discernment, the reverse is actually true.

Unless we are seeing through the eyes of God's love, we are not seeing clearly, and we will not accurately interpret what we see.

True discernment can only operate through God's love. This love is not to be confused with unsanctified mercy, which gives approval to the things of which God disapproves. Even though God's love is utterly pure and easily distinguishes between the pure and the impure, it does so for the right reasons. Insecurity, self-preservation, self-promotion, unhealed wounds, unfor-giveness, bitterness, etc., will all confuse and neutralize true spiritual discernment.

Spiritual Maturity

Almost everyone in ministry must endure considerable rejection and misunderstanding. Learning to overcome rejection, by forgiving and praying for our persecutors just as the Lord did, is essential if we are to walk in the Spirit and exercise true spiritual authority. If we are to accomplish the purposes of God, we must come to the level of maturity where, **"the love of Christ controls us" (II Corinthians 5:14).** Love does not take into account the wrongs we have suffered and is not motivated by rejection, which drives us to retaliate or to try to prove ourselves. Such reactions are the first step in a fall from true authority. As the Lord Jesus stated,

> **"He who speaks from himself seeks his own glory** [literally "recognition"]; **but He who is seeking the glory** [recognition] **of the One who sent Him, He is true, and there is no unrighteousness in Him" (John 7:18).**

seek God's Glory

There are few things that will more quickly destroy our ability to walk in true spiritual authority than self-seeking, self-promotion, or self-preservation. Learning to deal with rejection is mandatory if we are to walk in a true ministry. Rejection provides an opportunity for us to grow in grace and die a little more to ambition, pride, and other motives which so quickly color our revelation. If we embrace rejection as the discipline of the Lord, we will grow in grace and love. If we rebel against this discipline, we may enter into witchcraft. *Embrace rejection!*

The Fear of Man Leads to Witchcraft

King Saul is a good example of how a man with a true commission from God can fall into this counterfeit spiritual authority. When Saul was commanded to wait for Samuel before offering the sacrifice, he succumbed to pressure and offered it prematurely, saying,

"I saw that the people were scattering from me...and that the Philistines were assembling..." (I Samuel 13:11). This is the same point where most who fall from true authority do so—when they begin to fear the people or the circumstances more than they fear God. When we start to fear the people leaving more than we fear God leaving, we have departed from true faith.

Because witchcraft is basically rooted in the fear of man, and **"the fear of man brings a snare" (Proverbs 29:25),** those who begin to operate in witchcraft are trapped because fear has snared them. The bigger the project or ministry that we have built with hype, manipulation, or control spirits, the more we will most fear anyone or anything that we cannot manipulate or control. Those who are caught in this deadly trap will fear those who walk in the true anointing and authority. That is because those who walk in true spiritual authority are the least affected by the manipulation or spirit of control.

Saul became enraged at David and was consumed with destroying him, even though David was at the time but **"a single flea" (I Samuel 24:14).** As the manipulation and control spirits increase their dominion, so will the paranoia of those who are trapped in

14

their grasp. Such people will become irrationally consumed by an attempt to drive out or destroy anyone who threatens their control.

Those who receive their authority, recognition or security from men will, like Saul, end up in the witch's house, which is why Samuel warned Saul that **"rebellion is as the sin of witchcraft" (I Samuel 15:23 NKJV).** When one in spiritual authority rebels against the Holy Spirit, the void will be filled by the counterfeit spiritual authority of witchcraft. This may begin as a simple reliance upon hype and soul power, but without repentance it can end up in the most diabolical forms of presumption and rebellion, as we see in the case of King Saul. Persecuting those who were faithful to the Lord, Saul killed the true priests and spent one of his last nights in the house of a witch as the natural conclusion to the direction that his life had taken.

Spiritual authority is a dangerous occupation. If we are wise, like David, we will not seek a position of authority, and we will not even take one which is offered until we are certain that the Lord is the One giving it. Satan tempts every one called by God with the same temptation he offered to Jesus—if we will bow down to him and his ways, he will give us authority over kingdoms. God has called us to rule over kingdoms too, but His way leads to the cross. The authority He offers us can only be attained if we become servants of all. Satan's temptation is to offer the quick and easy path to the same place to which God has in fact called us.

Presumption Kills

One of the most frequent phrases attributed to David's life was, **"David inquired of the Lord" (I Samuel 30:8).** On the few occasions when David made a major decision without inquiring of the Lord, the consequences were devastating. The higher the position of authority, the more dangerous it is and the more people are affected by even seemingly insignificant decisions. True spiritual authority is not an honor to be sought; it is a burden to be carried. Many who seek authority and influence do not know what they are asking for. Immaturity can be our doom if authority is given to us before our time.

Even though David lived a thousand years before the age of grace, he knew the Lord's grace and lived by it. Yet, he still made mistakes which cost thousands of lives. It was probably because Solomon had observed this in his father that the one thing he desired was wisdom to rule over God's people. Anyone called to a position of leadership in the church must have the same devotion. Even if we are not in a position of spiritual authority, presumption can kill us. If we are in a position of authority, presumption will almost certainly lead to our fall, and can lead to the fall of many others as well.

The gift of a word of knowledge can be an awesome demonstration of power, but those who are called to walk in spiritual authority would do well to seek words of wisdom even more than words of knowledge. We need demonstrations of power and words of knowledge to accomplish the work of the Lord, but it is essential that we also have the wisdom to use them properly.

Humility Is a Safety Net

Those who attain prominence before humility will almost certainly fall. Therefore, if we have wisdom, we will seek humility before position. True authority operates on the grace of God, and the more authority we walk in, the more grace we will need. *We only have true spiritual authority to the degree that the King lives within us.* True spiritual authority is not position; it is grace. Counterfeit spiritual authority stands on its position instead of grace. Jesus is the highest spiritual authority, and He used His position to lay down His life. He commanded those who would come after Him to take up their crosses and do the same (see Matthew 16:24).

There is a simple distinguishing factor between the false prophets and the true. False prophets use their gifts and the people for themselves. True prophets use their gifts and give themselves for the people. Again, self-seeking, self-promotion, and self-preservation are the most destructive forces to true ministry. Like King Saul, even if we have been anointed by God, we can fall to witchcraft if these forces gain control over us.

Protection from Charismatic Witchcraft

Not only must those in leadership be wary of using witchcraft, they must also be aware that they will be the primary target of those who do. Witchcraft therefore is an enemy we must guard against from within and without. It is just as subtle when it attacks from without as when it takes ground from within. This form of sorcery is seldom what we call black magic, but is usually a form of "white witchcraft." Those who practice it are often well-meaning people who do not have the confidence to be straight-forward, and have therefore fallen to subtle forms of manipulation to gain influence.

18

One prominent form of white witchcraft, which is common in the church, can be described as "charismatic witchcraft." This is a pseudo-spirituality used to gain influence or control by wearing a super-spiritual mask. This is a source of false prophecies, dreams, and visions which ultimately destroy or neutralize a church, or bring the leadership to the point where they overreact so as to despise prophecy altogether. Those using this form of witchcraft will almost always think that they have the mind of the Lord, and therefore conclude that the leadership are the ones in rebellion.

Jezebel

Jezebel, who is one of the archetypes of witchcraft in Scripture, used her power to control her husband, who had the authority over Israel. She was also able to bring such depression upon Elijah that he sought death over life, even after his greatest spiritual victory. There is great power in this evil. Those who are ignorant of it, or who presumptuously disregard its potential to affect them, are very often brought down by it, usually without ever knowing what hit them.

Ahab may have easily been overpowered, but Elijah was certainly no wimp. He had just single-handedly confronted and destroyed more than eight hundred false prophets. This was one of the greatest demonstrations of God's power over evil in all of history, yet after this, one woman operating in the power of witchcraft was able to send the great prophet fleeing in discouragement.

How could this happen? Compared to the power of God, all the power of the evil one would not even register on the scale! The newest babe in Christ has more power dwelling in him than all of the antichrists put together. How is it that we are still overcome by evil? It is because Satan does not confront God's people with power; *he seduces them with deception.* Satan seduces us deception.

Compared to the eight hundred false prophets, who was this one woman to challenge Elijah? Certainly he could have destroyed her power even more easily than he had destroyed the power of the false prophets. It was not rational for Elijah to have become so discouraged because of Jezebel's threat, but that is precisely the point. This attack did not come through reasoning; it was a spiritual attack. Reasoning usually has little to do with the power of witchcraft.

Jezebel slammed Elijah immediately after his greatest victory, and he was overpowered. We will often be most vulnerable to this attack after a great victory because it is then that we tend to drop our guard and be the most open to pride. So, our first defense against the attacks of the enemy through witchcraft or any other tactic, is to maintain the humility of knowing that we are standing only by God's grace. Pride leaves a breach in our armor that the enemy can easily penetrate.

*We stand only by God's grace!

Part II

The Stinger

The attacks of witchcraft come in a series of stings. The successive stings are meant to hit the very places where we have been weakened by the previous stings. In this way they build upon each other until the cumulative effect overwhelms the target. The stings of witchcraft usually come in the following order:

1. **Discouragement**
2. **Confusion**
3. **Depression**
4. **Loss of Vision**
5. **Disorientation**
6. **Withdrawal**
7. **Despair**
8. **Defeat**

This process can happen quickly, as it did with Elijah, but it usually works more slowly, which makes it even more difficult to discern. However, if we know the enemy's schemes we will not continue to be subject to them. When these symptoms begin to make inroads into our lives, we must resist the enemy until he flees. If we do not resist him, we will be the ones fleeing, just like Elijah.

The source of witchcraft used against us may not be the obvious satanic cults or New Age operatives. It can come from well-meaning, though deceived, Christians who are, in effect, praying against us instead of for us. These misguided prayers have power because whatever is released on earth is released in heaven, and whatever is bound on earth is bound in heaven (see Matthew 16:19). If intercession is motivated by a spirit of control or manipulation, it is witchcraft and its power is just as real as that of black magic.

Other sources of charismatic witchcraft can be such things as gossip, political maneuvering, and jealousy; and they can have an effect on us whether we allow ourselves to be manipulated by them or not. For example, consider the result if we refuse to be manipulated by someone who has a control spirit, but allow ourselves to become resentful or bitter toward that person. In such a case, the enemy has still caused us to fall, and the discouragement, disorientation, and depression will come upon us just as surely as if we had submitted to the control spirit.

We are defeated by the enemy when he can get us to respond in any spirit other than the Holy Spirit, whose fruit is love, joy, peace, etc. (see Galatians 5:22-23). The enemy's strategy is to cause us to depart from the fruit of the Holy Spirit and try to combat him on his own terms. Satan cannot cast out Satan; resentment will never cast out Jezebel—it will only increase her power.

That is why the basic strategy we must use to begin freeing ourselves from the power of witchcraft is to *bless those who curse us* (see Luke 6:28). This does not mean that we bless their works, but that we pray for them and not against them. If the enemy can get us to retaliate, he will then have us using the same spirit and we will have multiplied the very evil we were trying to cast out.

We are not warring against flesh and blood, and the weapons of our warfare are not carnal but spiritual. When we begin to pray blessings upon the people who are attacking us, then the evil power of control and manipulation is broken over both them and us. We must not return evil for evil, but we must **"overcome evil with good" (Romans 12:21).**

Discerning the Stings of Witchcraft

Sting 1—DISCOURAGEMENT

Everyone gets discouraged at times, and it can be for many different reasons, so this is not always the result of witchcraft being used against us. But if we become subject to increasing discouragement for no apparent reason, witchcraft should be considered as a possible source. When your difficulties seem insurmountable and you want to give up, even though matters are really not any worse than usual, you are probably coming under spiritual attack. The enemy's attempt to afflict you with discouragement is meant to weaken you for the next level of attack, which is:

Sting 2—CONFUSION

Again, we must look for a general and increasing "spirit of confusion" for which there is no apparent reason. Here we begin to lose our clarity as to what we have been called to do, which of course will weaken our resolve. This confusion is meant to compound our discouragement, making us even weaker and more vulnerable to further attack, which will usually come in the form of:

Sting 3—DEPRESSION

This is a deeper problem than simple discouragement. It is an unshakable dread that comes as a result of the combined effect of discouragement and confusion, along with a general negligence in spiritual disciplines that has usually slipped in by this time. This will become an increasingly prevalent problem in the last days, and we must gain the victory over it. If we do not, it will quickly lead to the next sting:

Sting 4—LOSS OF VISION

This is the goal of the previous stings, and it works to increase their effect. Here we begin to doubt that God has called us to the task in the first place. The only way we can sail through the storm of confusion is to hold our course, but we cannot hold our course if we do not know where we are going. We will not try to hold our course if we begin to think it was wrong for us to ever pursue our vision in the first place. Such a loss in vision will lead to our drifting in circles at the time when we most need to **"make straight paths for your feet" (Hebrews 12:13).** This sets us up for the next level of assault:

Sting 5—DISORIENTATION

The combined result of depression, confusion, and loss of vision is usually disorientation. By this time, not only have we forgotten the course we are supposed to be holding, but we have even lost our ability to read the compass. The Scriptures will no longer speak to us, and it is a struggle to trust the Lord's voice or receive much encour-agement from even the most anointed teaching or preaching. This is the point of spiritual incapacitation, the inability to function, which results in:

Sting 6—WITHDRAWAL

When disorientation sets in, it is tempting to withdraw or retreat from our purpose in the ministry, our fellowship with the rest of the church, and often from our families and others that we are close to. Withdrawal will result in:

Sting 7—DESPAIR

Withdrawal from the battle leads quickly to hopelessness and despair. Without hope we can easily be taken out by the enemy, either through temptation, sickness, or death. Science has proven that when hope is removed, even the most healthy person will quickly deteriorate and die. But with hope, men and women have lived long past the point when a normal body would have quit. Despair will always lead to:

Sting 8—DEFEAT.

The enemy's purpose is to weaken us so we will begin to fall further and further behind—then we can be picked off more easily. In Scripture the Amalekites were typical of Satan and his hordes. It was the practice of the Amalekites to attack the weak and the defenseless. As the camp of Israel crossed the wilderness, the Amalekites picked off the loners or stragglers who fell behind the rest of the camp.

This is what the enemy seeks to do through witchcraft. He seeks to weaken believers so that they will begin to fall behind the rest of the camp and become easy prey. This is why Israel was told that there would be a perpetual war with the Amalekites. When Israel's kings were commanded to fight them, they were also commanded to utterly destroy them and not take any spoil. We have a perpetual war against Satan, and we cannot take any prisoners. Neither can we use that which is his in the service of God.

King Saul disobeyed this command. He kept Agag alive, king of the Amalekites, and kept some of the spoil **"to sacrifice it to the Lord" (I Samuel 15:15).** This represented a failure of the most foolish kind for one called to lead God's people. In those days, keeping a rival king alive after a battle was only done for one of two reasons: to make him an ally or a slave. Saul foolishly thought that he could make the one who personified Satan himself into an ally or a slave.

It was no accident that it was an Amalekite who killed Saul and carried the news of Saul's death to David. This Amalekite thought that the news would be pleasing to David, but David was discerning and had him killed (see

30

II Samuel 1:1-16). If we do not obey the Lord and utterly destroy the enemy we battle, he will end up finishing us off. There can be no alliance with the enemy; he and his hordes must be utterly destroyed. Neither let us be foolish enough to think that we can use the enemy as our slave; in his guile he will quickly turn the tables. *You can't enslave the enemy.*

Witchcraft is being used against the church. Many who have failed to recognize it have been defeated, losing their vision, their ministry, their families, and even their lives. This is not sensationalism; it is fact. Paul said that we do not wrestle against flesh and blood, but against principalities and powers (see Ephesians 6:12). Wrestling is the closest form of combat. The enemy is going to fight, and he is going to wrestle with us. If we decide that we are just not going to fight, we will get pinned!

As Christians, we have no option as to whether or not we are going to do spiritual warfare—if we want to survive, we must fight. But how do we combat this witchcraft? We must first look at the basic principle of spiritual warfare required for every victory.

The Road to Victory

In Revelation 12:11 we see that the saints overcome Satan:

1. By the blood of the Lamb,
2. By the word of their testimony, and
3. By loving not their lives even unto death.

We overcome by the blood of the Lamb as we take our stand on what He has already accomplished for us by the cross. The victory has already been won and there is no way we can lose, if we abide in Him.

The word of our testimony is the Scriptures. Every time the enemy challenged Jesus, He simply responded with Scripture, countering the enemy's temptation with God's truth. The Word of God is **"the sword of the Spirit" (Ephesians 6:17).** With the sword we can deflect the blows from his deceptive words, as well as attack him. Of all the pieces of armor we are commanded to use, the sword is the only offensive weapon (see Ephesians 6:10-18).

That they **"did not love their life even to death" (Revelation 12:11),** is the utter commitment to follow Him regardless of the price. We are called to take up our crosses daily, to do all things for the sake of the gospel, and to no longer live for ourselves but for Him. To the degree we remain in self-centeredness, we will be vulnerable to the enemy's attack. When we have reckoned ourselves dead to this world, as crucified with

Christ, then the enemy no longer has any access to us because he has no more access to Him. If we are dead to this world, what can be done to a dead person? It is impossible for the dead to be offended, to be tempted, to fear, to be depressed, or to be continually looking for the easy way out, since they have already paid the ultimate price. *Become dead to self.*

All of these—the blood of the Lamb, the word of our testimony, and a commitment to lay down our lives, are required for spiritual victory. Anything less will fail to bring a complete victory. We may make occasional, halting advances, but we will sooner or later be pushed back. However, it is clear that at the end of the age an army of believers will be raised up who will not settle for occasional advances—they will have committed themselves to the fight and will not stop until there is total victory. **"The earth is the Lord's, and all it contains" (Psalm 24:1).** Until the earth has been completely recovered from the domain of Satan, our fight is not over.

No one will fight to win if he or she do not believe victory is possible. Many teachings have been promulgated that declare the church's defeat before Christ's return. Yet the whole prophetic testimony of Scripture is that the Lord, the church, and the truth are going to prevail. Satan is indeed being cast down to the earth, bringing with him a time of trouble like the world has never known before—but we will still win!

Isaiah 14:16-17 states that when we see Satan we are going to marvel at the pitiful nature of the one who caused so much trouble! He who lives within the very least of the saints is much greater than the combined power of all antichrists. These times are not to be feared—this will be our finest hour! As Isaiah 60:1-2 declares, when darkness is covering the earth, the glory of the Lord will be appearing on His people. The darkness will just make His glory upon us appear that much brighter. We must start fighting in order to win, giving no more ground to the enemy and taking back what he has usurped.

To effectively combat witchcraft, we must determine that we are going to resist Satan until he flees from us. Our goal is more than just driving the enemy out of our own lives; we then must pursue him until he is driven out of others in whom he has established a stronghold. The following are some of the ways we can combat and overcome eight specific areas of Satan's attack through witchcraft.

1. Overcoming Discouragement

Discouragement never comes from God. He is the author of faith and the source of

OPPOSITE of Discouragement is Faith

hope which never disappoints. Although God disciplines us when we need it, He never does so by afflicting us with discouragement. When James describes the wisdom that comes from above, he does not list discouragement as one of the characteristics. **"But the wisdom from above is first pure, then peaceable, gentle, reasonable, full of mercy and good fruits, unwavering, without hypocrisy" (James 3:17).** Discouragement is the very opposite of love, joy, peace, and other attributes of the Holy Spirit's fruit (see Galatians 5:22-23).

We must learn to quickly and instinctively reject discouragement, giving it no place in our thoughts. We must tenaciously resist it, taking every thought captive to obey Christ (see II Corinthians 10:3). Discouragement must never be allowed to dictate our course. *Faith* is the fruit of the Spirit and the shield of our armor that counters discouragement. If we begin to get discouraged, it is because we have dropped our shield. We need to pick it back up!

2. Overcoming Confusion

"God is not the author of confusion" (I Corinthians 14:33 KJV), so we can know for certain that when confusion strikes, it is not coming from Him. In the military, confusion is one of the primary elements of battle that a soldier is trained to handle. Since nothing will ever go exactly as planned, there will rarely be a battle where there is not confusion. The same is true in spiritual warfare.

The disciplined soldier who understands this aspect of warfare learns to use the confusion to his own advantage. He does not let it increase his discouragement, but begins to anticipate it, looking for an opportunity to gain an advantage over the enemy. We must learn to expect confusion as part of the battle and not be surprised or affected by it. Our resolve to stand and fight will quickly dispel this aspect of the attack.

3. Overcoming Depression

God told Cain the most effective remedy for depression:

> **Then the LORD said to Cain, "Why are you angry? And why has your countenance fallen** [the ancient expression for depression]?
>
> *If you do well, will not your countenance be lifted up?* **And if you do not do well, sin is crouching at the door; and its desire is for you, but you must master it" (Genesis 4:6-7** emphasis mine).

Depression is usually the result of allowing discouragement and confusion to cause us to drift from our basic spiritual disciplines, such as reading the Word, praying, fellowshipping, etc. Picking them up again with resolve will almost always start to reverse the downward spiral. [Fellowship]

4. Overcoming a Loss of Vision

This attack can also be turned to our advantage and used as an opportunity. When we begin to lose our vision, we must commit ourselves to strengthening our vision more than ever. We need to sink our roots deeper and establish our purpose even more firmly upon the Word of God. When God begins to lead us into a purpose, we should record how He speaks to us. By searching all the Scriptures and reviewing the ways He has led us in the past, we will even more firmly establish His leading.

Above all, we must hold our course! We should not change our direction until we can clearly see the new course. In World War I, one of the most effective tactics of the enemy was to lay a smokescreen in front of allied battleship convoys. As the convoy entered the smoke, visibility was lost. The ships would start turning at any perceived sound or whim with the resulting collisions sinking more ships than the enemy torpedoes did.

The allies finally developed a simple strategy to thwart this tactic against their vision: When in the smoke, every ship was to hold its previous course without deviation. By doing so, they discovered that they would soon all sail out the other side into clear air. The same strategy will enable us to more quickly escape whatever is clouding our vision. When we lose our vision, we need to just hold our course and keep going forward. We will soon break out into the clear.

5. Overcoming Disorientation

As an instrument flight instructor, the first thing I had to teach a student pilot was that he must not trust his feelings when experiencing restricted visibility while flying on instruments. If a pilot tries to fly by his feelings when in instrument conditions, he will quickly lose control of the plane. Even when flying perfectly straight and level through the clouds, it can begin to feel like the plane is turning. If the pilot reacts to this feeling, he will begin to turn in order to counteract this supposed drift, causing the plane to veer off course or possibly even turn the plane upside down.

In a test conducted by the FAA, a group of pilots without previous instrument training were flown into instrument conditions. Every one of them lost control of their planes because they tried to rely on their feelings for guidance. The same is true of immature Christians who enter spiritual conditions of reduced visibility or "spiritual clouds." They usually try to rely on their feelings for guidance and therefore lose control.

The "instruments" we have been given to walk by are found in the Bible. We do not walk by feelings but by faith in the sure testimony of the Word of God. The Word of God will keep us oriented and on course if we put our trust in it, even when our feelings may be telling us to do otherwise.

6. Overcoming Withdrawal

In the Persian Gulf War, the majority of casualties were either reserves or civilians. The safest place to be in the war was on the front line. This has been true in most modern wars, and it is true in spiritual warfare as well.

When you're being pressed in a battle, you cannot call a time-out. On the front line we cannot ask the enemy to stop the battle because we have a headache or want to take a break. When we are on the front line, we know the dangers and do not let our guard down.

Every Christian is on the front line every day whether he likes it or not. Satan will not stop when we call a time-out. It is when we start to consider ourselves a "civilian" or not a soldier, that we will be the most vulnerable to his attack. A Christian is never in the reserves, but there are times of reprieve from conflict for seldom do battles continually rage along the entire front. However, when we know we are on the front, even our breaks are taken with vigilance, realizing that a fresh attack can come at any time. Christians must never remove their spiritual armor, and must never lose their vigilance.

In time of warfare, there are occasions when strategic retreat is necessary. At times, we overcommited ourselves spiritually and must draw back—but that is not the same as withdrawing from the battle. Even when we have overcommitted ourselves, retreat should be a last resort, for an army in retreat is in its most vulnerable condition. If at all possible, we should at least try to hold our ground until our position can be strengthened.

Even when we discover that in a certain matter we have acted presumptuously, without being commissioned by God, we must not quit—we should repent. There is a difference between quitting and stopping because of repentance. The first is a defeat; the latter is an adjustment that will always result in further victories. Repentance comes because of the truth that sets us free; defeat will result in a spiritual bondage to the power of the enemy.

7. Overcoming Despair

In Genesis 2:18, the Lord said that it was not good for man to be alone. We are social creatures, and when we withdraw from fellowship we usually sink into the deepest pit of hopelessness—despair. At this point in the downward spiral, we must return to fellowship and get help in reversing the slide or else we will be defeated.

As simple as this may seem, *it is the remedy*. Even though fellow believers can be the source of the enemy's attack on us, we must never run away from the church. We should run to it and work out our problems until they are resolved.

8. Overcoming Defeat

Even if Satan's stings of witchcraft have brought such devastation to our lives that we are temporarily defeated, we must see that God can still bring us to ultimate victory. Paul commented to the Corinthians that he had been **"struck down, but not destroyed"** (**II Corinthians 4:9**). At one point, Paul faced such severe attacks that he **"despaired even of life" (II Corinthians 1:8)**, but through it all he learned that the secret of regaining victory was not in trusting in himself but in "God who raises the dead" (II Corinthians 1:9).

Paul wrote, **"thanks be to God, who gives us victory through our Lord Jesus Christ"** (I Corinthians 15:57) and **"But in all these things we overwhelmingly conquer through Him who loved us"** (Romans 8:37). Defeat is not an option in Christ. We will gain victory in that which He has called us to do. The only way we can be defeated is to quit.

Part III

Combating New Age Witchcraft

The New Age movement is basically a combination of witchcraft and Hinduism, disguised to make it acceptable to white-collar professionals. There is an important reason why this form of spiritualism is targeting this group. For almost 5,800 years of the earth's 6,000 years of recorded history, nearly 95 percent of all workers were agricultural. In just a little over a century, that statistic has been reversed so that now less than 5 percent of the workers in the West are agricultural. This change was the result of technological advances. The 5 percent who work in agri-culture now produce more than the 95 percent could in the last century.

In the mid 1950s, white-collar workers exceeded the number of blue-collar workers in the West. Since that time, this majority has grown until it is now estimated that blue-collar workers will go the way of agricultural workers in the near future, composing only a very small fraction of population. When it was predicted that **"knowledge will increase"** (**Daniel 12:4**) in the end times, few could have comprehended the degree to which this would happen. Information is now the most valuable commodity in the world, and the job of accumulating, interpreting, packaging, and transferring knowledge is the largest industry.

Those involved in the "knowledge industry" are not only the most numerous, they are also the wealthiest and most powerful. They are also a group that the church has become increasingly unsuccessful in reaching, which has made them an appealing target for the New Age movement and other cults. Man was created to have fellowship with God, who is Spirit, and because of this there is a spiritual void in man that hungers for the supernatural.

The day of supernatural neutrality is over. Those who do not know the true supernatural power of God will become increasingly subject to the evil and counterfeit supernatural powers of the enemy. Those whose fears or doctrines have led them to avoid the supernatural power of God will find themselves, and especially their children, easy prey to evil, supernatural power.

Kingdoms in Conflict

Paul explained, **"For the kingdom of God does not consist in words, but in power" (I Corinthians 4:20).** Satan knows this, and is therefore quite content to fight the battle on the level of words and doctrines. Regardless of how accurately we can argue doctrinal positions, Satan will have little problem conquering us if we do not know the power of God, which is a fundamental aspect of God's kingdom! Those who really believe the Bible will walk in power. Righteousness is the result of believing in our hearts, not just in our minds, and those who do not know the power of God are only believing Him in their minds.

Considering the foolish antics that often zing those of us who have known the power of God in the Pentecostal, Charismatic, Full Gospel, and the Third Wave movements, it is easy to understand why many would shy away from the gifts of the Spirit. But this, too, is one of the tests that separate the true believers from those who just know creeds or doctrines. God has called the foolish things of the world to confound the wise. Only the humble will come to what He is doing, and He will give His grace only to them.

Churches which have rejected the supernatural power of God have become increasingly irrelevant and unable to reach the world, for the battle for men's souls is intensely supernatural in nature. The more secularized society becomes, the more it actually magnifies people's hunger for the supernatural. That is why atheists tend to be drawn to the most base forms of witchcraft and the black arts, which they are deceived into thinking are powers resident within man, when actually the powers are demonic in nature. The denominations and movements within the church that have rejected the power of God are almost all shrinking because they have become irrelevant and boring, with little or no power to attract converts.

Many of the churches and denominations that have rejected the power of God have already succumbed to influences from the New Age movement. Others are succumbing to the spirit of the age in other forms, not only tolerating the perverted and unbelievers as members, but actually ordaining them as pastors and leaders. Contrary to this, the denominations and movements that preach and walk in the supernatural power of God are not only growing, but are by far the fastest growing religious movements in the world.

Paul the apostle declared:

And my message and my preaching were not in persuasive words of wisdom, but in demonstration of the Spirit and of powers,

that your faith should not rest on the wisdom of men, but on the power of God **(I Corinthians 2:4-5** emphasis mine).

The conflict between the kingdom of God and the kingdom of evil is not just a conflict between truth and error (though it is that too), it is a confrontation of supernatural powers, with both sides seeking to fill the spiritual void in man created by the Fall.

The entire history of God's dealings with mankind have involved demonstrations of supernatural power. It is incongruous to say we are a biblical people and yet not walk in the supernatural power of God. True Christianity is not just a matter of words; it is a demonstration of God's love and power to save, heal, and deliver. Jesus stated that as the Father had sent Him into the world, He has sent us into the world (see John 17:18). As our example, Jesus did not just talk about God's power to heal and save, He demonstrated it.

If we are going to preach the gospel, we must preach it as He did, demonstrating both God's love and His power. When Jesus sent out His disciples to preach the kingdom, they were to heal the sick and cast out demons (see Luke 9:1-2). The Lord never changes nor does He change the way He sends His true messengers.

Many of the biblical prophecies concerning the end of the age address the supernatural nature of the conflicts that will occur. A church that does not walk in God's power will become increasingly inadequate to deal with the times and confront the powers that come against it. To overcome the increasing power of the enemy we must **"desire earnestly spiritual gifts, but especially that** [we] **may** prophesy" (I Corinthians 14:1). "God is spirit, and those who worship Him must worship in spirit and truth" (John 4:24). Again, the first defense against the deceptive supernatural power of the enemy is to know the true power of God.

Most believers have *some* desire for spiritual gifts, but we must *"earnestly"* desire them if we are going to receive them. Even though most of the church is now "open" for God to use them in a demonstration of His power, He has decreed that we must *ask, seek, and knock* in order to receive (see Matthew 7:7). Those who are just "open" for the Lord to use them are rarely used. Being "open" is usually a cop-out for those who are either too fearful or too prideful to risk failure. It takes faith and persistent seeking if we are to receive.

Pious Delusions

It is often repeated that we are to seek the Giver and not the gifts. That sounds pious, but it is not biblical. Certainly we are to seek the Giver more than the gifts, but we are commanded to seek the gifts, too. The two are not mutually exclusive. Seeking to walk in the gifts of the Spirit is actually one form of seeking God, and even more important, it is being obedient. Many such glib statements of apparent wisdom are merely human wisdom, and are often in conflict with the Scriptures.

Our God is supernatural, and we cannot truly desire fellowship with Him without desiring fellowship with the supernatural. While many Christians have been hardened by doctrines that justify their powerlessness, claiming that God no longer moves supernaturally, even those believers long in their hearts for the supernatural. We were all created for fellowship in the Spirit, which is by definition supernatural.

Recently, some of the world's most brilliant theologians and apologists, who believed God no longer worked supernaturally, have been won over and are now walking in God's power themselves, often after witnessing just one genuine miracle. *"Genuine"* is the key word here. Those who sincerely love God and seek to walk in His power are turned off by the fakery and hype often associated with the ministries of those who really do not yet have God's power.

The True Gospel

True Christianity is the true Word of God verified by the true power of God. Jesus went about to **"do and teach" (Acts 1:1)**. He usually performed miracles *before* He taught. He knew that people who have an undeniable

50

encounter with God are going to be far more open to what He would say to them. The power Jesus and His apostles demonstrated was used to confirm and illuminate their teachings.

The same is still true. The demonstration of God's power transforms intellectual concepts into a true faith in the teachings of the Lord. It takes both the Word and the power of God to change the inner man. Without both, we may change our outward behavior, but our hearts remain untouched. It is the spiritual void in the heart that must be filled by a true fellowship with God if we are going to be free from the spiritual influence and power of the enemy.

Because witchcraft is counterfeit spiritual authority, we will only be completely free from the power of witchcraft when we are completely submitted to the authority of God. If the spiritual void that is in us is not filled with the real power and authority of God, we will become subject to witchcraft in some form as we draw closer to the end of the age. The Battle of Armageddon is fought in the **"valley of decision" (Joel 3:14);** everyone on earth will be brought to the place of making a decision. It is a power confrontation, and the choice is being made concerning issues of power and authority. We will choose either the power and authority of God, or the power and authority of the evil one—but we will all choose.

Discerning Counterfeits

All of the spiritual gifts available to the church are presently being counterfeited by the enemy. Ironically, those whose lack of faith causes them to avoid spiritual gifts in order to keep from being deceived, are *certain* to be deceived. We must walk by faith, not fear, if we are going to stay on the path that leads to life. Fear will inevitably lead us to deception if we allow it to be our motivation. If we are going to fufill the purpose of God, it will take a faith like Abraham's, willing to risk leaving everything behind in order to seek that which He is building. If we are going to walk in the power of God, we must have more faith in God to lead us into all truth than we do in the enemy's ability to deceive us. Faith is the door to fellowship with God, because it takes faith to reach beyond the natural realm to the supernatural, so that we can see **"Him who is unseen" (Hebrews 11:27).**

As we walk in faith, that which we begin to see with the eyes of our hearts will become more real to us than what we are seeing with our natural eyes. Then we will begin living more for the eternal than for the temporal.

Those who walk in true faith are naturally going to appear foolish to those who live according to the wisdom of this world or those who are of a "natural mind."

We take a major step in being delivered from the power of witchcraft when we start to see the Lord so clearly that we respect and serve Him more than anything else. Then we are no longer subject to the influence, manipulation, and control of those who are still earthly minded, or who move in the power of witchcraft.

Those who give themselves to becoming authorities on the nature of evil almost always become darkened and evil in nature themselves. Many "cult watchers" have released a more foul spirit in the church than the cults they were watching. The paranoia they have promulgated has done more to bring division and damage to the church than any cult has been able to do. These have often become the "faultfinders" that Jude talked about (see Jude 16), printing and distributing slander and gossip as if it were researched fact. As Jude warned, these are being reserved for the **"black darkness" (Jude 13)**, in which many of them have already begun to live.

We do not need to study the darkness as much as we need to study the light. Light will always overpower darkness. If we walk in the light, we will cast out the darkness. If we walk in the true supernatural power of God, we will overpower the evil supernatural power as surely as Moses confounded the sorcerers of Egypt. But Moses would not have been successful had he gone to Egypt with no power, and neither will we succeed in setting people free today if we are powerless. The increasing power of the enemy will not be effectively confronted and driven out without the power of God.

The Enemy's Strategy

Most of the cults and New Age groups are now blatantly attacking Christianity, focusing on the church as the main target of their sorcery. Not only are they infiltrating the church, but they are using their power to cast spells on those in ministry. In my book, *The Harvest*, I wrote about cult members entering church meetings and performing lewd acts to intimidate and humiliate believers, and this has already begun to happen with alarming frequency.

There is a simple solution for churches that have become the target of such attacks—they must seek to know and walk in God's authority and power. He who is in us is much greater than he who is in the world (see I John 4:4). As the church grows in true spiritual authority, the cults are going to start fearing us far more than we fear them.

Sorcerers usually try to avoid direct confrontation with those who have true spiritual authority. Although they will attack those who are growing in spiritual authority and bearing fruit for the kingdom of God, this is generally not done openly but in secret. The attacks are done indirectly by sacrificing and cursing according to the black arts.

We must recognize the power in satanic sacrifices if we are going to overcome it. In II Kings 3:27, the king of Moab offered his oldest son as a burnt offering to his demon gods and as a result, **"there came a great wrath against Israel, and they departed..."** (from attacking Moab). It is not biblical for a Christian to fear the enemy, but if we do not understand and properly respect his power, we will be vulnerable to its influence.

When combating evil powers we cannot come with carnal weapons or mere human strength—neither can we fight on Satan's terms. His first strategy in a confrontation is to get us out of the Holy Spirit's control and into a spirit of retaliation. We cannot overcome evil with evil; Satan will not cast out Satan. Jesus said, **"if I cast out demons by** the Spirit of God, then the kingdom of God has come upon you" (Matthew 12:28).

This is why Jesus commanded us to **"bless those who curse you"** (Luke 6:28). Blessings are more powerful than any curse and will quickly overcome them. Even so, it is important for us to recognize when we are being cursed with witchcraft, so that we can defend against it and shine light into the darkness that has been directed against us.

Summary

Witchcraft is basically the practice of cursing others. This cursing does not just come through cults or black magic arts, but can even come through those who love us and have good intentions, but are trying to manipulate us. Using manipulation or a control spirit is a from or witchcraft, regardless of who does it.

The mother who manipulates her son or daughter into marrying *her* choice has done it through witchcraft, and such relationships usually have to be held together through manipulation and control. The prayer group that uses prayers to expose others is gossiping for the sake of manipulation. This is not genuine prayer—it is witchcraft. Much of what is written in the name of Christian journalism purportedly as an attempt to keep the church informed, is gossip, used to manipulate or gain influence over others—this, too, is witchcraft.

When spiritual leaders who use manipulation, hype, or control to build their churches or ministries, they are operating in a counterfeit spiritual authority equivalent to witchcraft. Much of what is taught in business schools is a form of manipulation or control that is witchcraft. Many of the strategies the church has borrowed from secular journalism and the business world have brought witchcraft into the camp, and it must be removed if we are to be free to accomplish our purpose for this hour.

Many of the "yokes" and human expectations that we face have some power of manipulation and witchcraft attached to them. The enemy wants to establish these strongholds to conflict with the calling of God in our lives. However, this is not a license to disregard the expectations of our parents, teachers, employers, etc. We were known by the Lord before we were born, and many of the influences in our lives have been placed there to help steer us toward our purposes in Him. But some of the yokes and expectations that well-intentioned parents, teachers, or coaches put on us must be cast off. When yokes are placed on us that are not from the Lord, they will become clear as we come to know our calling and purpose in Him, for the truth will set us free.

The only yoke that we must take is the Lord's yoke. His yoke is easy and His burden is light (see Matthew 11:28-30). When we take His yoke we find rest and refreshment instead of the pressure and discouragement that came from white witchcraft. Pressure tactics and manipulation are subtle forms of witchcraft that can have just as much power as the black magic arts. White and black witchcraft may be different branches, but they have the same root and the same deadly poison.

Unfortunately, when unstable people recognize the dangers of being subject to charismatic or white witchcraft, they will often distort this principle in order to rebel against God's ordained authority over their lives. King Saul is a personification of one who was ordained by God but fell from his place of true spiritual authority to operate in counterfeit spiritual authority. King David, on the other hand, is a personification of true spiritual authority. How did David react to Saul? He was willing to serve in the house of Saul until Saul chased him away. Even then he never retaliated, rebelled, or tried to undermine Saul's authority;

but chose instead to honor him as **"the Lord's anointed"** (I Samuel 24:10).

We need to learn from David's example. Even though he was called to take Saul's place, he never lifted his hand against Saul. David determined that if God had really called him to be the next king, then God would have to be the One to establish him. David overcame evil with good by demonstrating the exact opposite of the manipulative or control spirits that had come against him. Had David manipulated his way into the kingdom, he would have almost certainly fallen to witchcraft just like Saul. But David was of a different spirit.

Those who are the target of any form of witchcraft will usually feel the sequence of stings previously listed. If we react to the attack properly, we will not only be free of its influence ourselves, but we can also help to free those who have used witchcraft. The manipulation and control spirits gain entrance through fear. Those who are fearful and insecure, and who are so obsessed with controlling others that they use evil influence, will take a demonstration of **"perfect love"** (I John 4:18) to cast out these fears. Jesus commanded us to **"bless those who curse you"** (Matthew 5:44 NKJV). Paul said that we are not to return evil for evil; we are to overcome evil with good (see Romans 12:19-21).

When we discover that we are the target of witchcraft, retaliation is not the answer. In fact, that is the very thing the enemy would have us do, for it multiplies the evil we are trying to cast out. Satan will not cast out Satan; witchcraft will not cast out witchcraft. We must pray for those who are praying against us and bless those who are cursing us. This does not mean we are to bless what they are *doing*, but we must pray that they are delivered from the fears and hatred that motivates them. Pray for your attackers to have a revelation of the perfect love of God. Our greatest victory is in winning those who are in the enemy's grip, not just in afflicting them back.

There is another source of witchcraft that can be one of the most unexpected causes of our discouragement, confusion, depression, loss of vision, disorientation and despair— *ourselves!* When we use manipulation, hype, or control on others, we open ourselves to the consequences. Before we look at others to find the source, we should first look at ourselves. Again, Satan cannot cast out Satan; we will not be able to cast witchcraft out of others if we are using it ourselves.

Most who have been subject to witchcraft have tried to combat it in the flesh, actually using the same spirit. When we do that, it gains a foothold in our own lives that must be broken before we will have the authority to deliver others.

Witchcraft is a serious offense that God will not continue to tolerate in the church. His intent is to bring down every form and manifestation of witchcraft that has ensnared His people. After we have been freed from this terrible evil, we will also be free to walk in the unprecedented power that can only be entrusted to those who walk in true spiritual authority.

Part IV

The Stronghold of Illegitimate Authority

In one of the most remarkable statements made in the New Testament, Peter wrote that we should be **"looking for and hastening the coming of the day of God" (II Peter 3:12).** Obviously, Peter would not have said this if it were not *possible* for us to hasten the coming of the day of God. But if we can hasten the coming of His day, it is apparent that we can also *delay* it. Because the enemy knows his time is short, we can also be sure that he will be doing all that he can to keep us from doing what will hasten the day of the Lord, and to keep us doing that which will cause its delay.

The harvest will come. It has already come to many parts of the world. Before the end, the Spirit will be poured out upon all flesh. However, there are major stumbling blocks to spiritual advancement that we must address if we are going to receive the full benefit of the impending awakening. These stumbling blocks are not big enough to stop revival altogether, but they can limit its scope, depth, duration, and fruit.

The harvest will bring the reaping of everything that has been sown, both good and evil. The harvest that marks the end of this age has already begun, but because many have the concept that the harvest is only a great revival, they do not see it or understand it. The Scriptures teach that the harvest will begin with the tares being taken out first (see Matthew 13:38-40, 49), and this has been going on for some time. In many ways it seems that we have *only* been reaping tares. This may be painful for a season, but this pain will be appreciated when the full harvest begins and we are able to avoid making the same mistakes again.

One aspect of the harvest of tares that had a significant impact on the international body of Christ came with the televangelist scandals of recent years. This is not to imply that the individuals involved were "tares," but the scandals that were brought to light began to uproot some erroneous practices and theologies. Unfortunately, these tares were not exposed by the church, but by the secular news media. As a friend remarked in a roundtable meeting that we hosted, "The Lord is using the secular media to discipline the church because we have refused to judge ourselves." There is an important truth to this observation.

That the Lord is using the secular media to discipline the church is a loud signal announcing our fallen condition. It is likewise apparent that much of the church has sincerely given herself to repentance. A sign that this repentance has been genuine enough to be acceptable to God will be when our sovereignty is restored—when the church is able to judge herself.

Even though the Lord used the heathen nations to discipline Israel for her apostasies, He afterward would often destroy those nations for their arrogance. This may shock our human sensibilities, but those heathen nations were still heathen. They still worshiped idols, and they would inevitably try to introduce their idol worship to Israel during their occupation.

The same has been happening between the secular media and the church. Much of the Christian media has been turning to the ways of the secular media. That is not the Lord's intended means for the church's discipline, and it will result in even worse consequences if we do not rid ourselves of it.

The Wrong Kind of Repentance

Journalism has crossed a line that has made it one of the primary platforms of the **"accuser of our brethren" (Revelation 12:10)**, and it has become a major stumbling block to spiritual advancement. This is no longer true of just secular journalism, for much of the Christian media has at times proven even less honorable and truthful in its reporting than the secular media.

Much more of the Christian media is now founded more upon a humanistic philosophy of journalism than upon biblical principles. Today the Christian media is one of the greatest sources of a deadly poison that is spreading destruction in the Western church—the spirit of *unrighteous judgment*. Although it is true that the Lord had to use the media because we would not judge ourselves, the solution to that is not for us to take on the ways of the heathen, but to return to God's righteous judgment as outlined in His Word.

There is a healthy skepticism that truly *wants* to believe, such as the Bereans displayed when they searched the Scriptures to verify the message of Paul and Barnabas (see Acts 17:11 NIV). However, there is another kind of skeptic that wants to *doubt*. This unhealthy form of skepticism wants to see the worst in others, because that somehow makes the skeptic look bigger or at least feel better about his own flaws.

This kind of doubt and cynicism is both tragic and deadly. When the chronicles of this earth are read on that great judgment day, we will probably learn that this evil form of doubt was far more deadly than cancer or AIDS. Great souls rise to even greater heights by lifting others higher. Criticism has an appearance of wisdom, but it is wisdom from the dark side, it is the fruit of the Tree of the Knowledge of Good and Evil.

Since the 1960s, the news media of the West, including the Christian media, seems to have been almost completely taken over by this dark side of skepticism. It is now almost unthinkable for a Christian journalist to write an article about a church, a movement, or an event, without at least throwing in some criticism. This is often done by reporting hearsay or crude gossip as fact, without the offended parties even having been contacted for their side of the story.

Those who simply pass on gossip are just as guilty of gossiping as those who originated it. All of this is usually done in the name of "the people's right to know," or "to protect people from error." But are we really protecting them from error when we do so by committing one of the most serious errors of all— becoming stumbling blocks?

The Scriptures are shockingly honest about exposing both the good qualities and the flaws in even the greatest spiritual heroes. Yet the Bible was written as history for the sake of instructing others in the ways of God, not for the sake of exposing dirt. How does today's Christian journalism justify it's departure from such biblical exhortations as these:

Let *no unwholesome word* proceed from your mouth, but only such a word as is good for edification according to the need of the moment, that it may give *grace* to those who hear (**Ephesians 4:29** emphasis mine).

"And if your brother sins, go and reprove him *in private*..." (**Matthew 18:15** emphasis mine).

In Matthew 18, the procedure for addressing sin was given to keep us from becoming stumbling blocks. Not following this procedure, especially in journalism, may have created more stumbling blocks to the Lord's own children than any other source. More damage has probably come to the church by such journalism and by so-called heresy hunting, than has come through the heresies they are trying to expose.

By What Authority?

Alexander Solzhenitsyn once said, "The press has become the greatest power within the Western countries, exceeding that of the legislature, the executive, and the judiciary. Yet one would like to ask: According to what law has it been elected and to whom is it responsible?" Solzhenitsyn's question is valid for Western society, but even more so for the church.

On what basis has the press been granted the extraordinary power it now has? By what authority has it been elected? The Lord appoints elders in the church to give it both protection and direction. He set high standards for those elders who would be given such influence. In contrast, to whom are the Christian journalists accountable, and to what standards must they be held? These are important questions.

Just as the secular media can now manipulate public opinion and dictate policy sometimes even more effectively than our elected officials, Christian journalists can do the same in the church. Who gave them this power? Is it derived merely from an ability to be articulate or because of the anointing and commission of God? Do we have the right to have a massive influence in the church simply because we have the marketing ability to distribute our magazines, newsletters, or programs?

James warned, **"Let not many of you become teachers, my brethren, knowing that as such we shall incur a stricter judgment"** **(James 3:1).** It is a most serious matter to have influence in the Lord's own household! Let us be very careful how we attain it and how we use it.

Paul explained that he did not presume to go beyond the sphere of authority that was appointed to him (see II Corinthians 10:14-18). He realized that God has given each of us certain realms of authority and grace, and we need to take care that we don't go beyond these appointed realms.

Where Are the Elders?

Much of what is done today by Christian journalism, and the heresy hunters, encroaches upon the realm of the authority that was given to the elders of the church. The very meaning of the word "elder" implied a certain degree of longevity in faithful service to the church before one was given this influence. The position of elder was the highest and most respected office appointed in the biblical church.

Journalists today, on the other hand, are often not accountable to anyone but an editor. Even though they are not required to comply with any of the biblical standards for leadership in the church, they can have more influence through the media than even the most anointed true elders.

Writing can be an aspect of a biblical ministry, and there are journalists who have obvious spiritual ministries as teachers, pastors, etc. Some of these have been faithful to the biblical standards required for leaders in the church, and they should be recognized as elders in the body of Christ. For such people, journalism can be a proper platform for the authority they have been given by God. Even so, they, too, can become stumbling blocks if they do not comply with the biblical procedures for bringing correction in the church.

Most of those who are the sources of the prevailing critical spirit, or spirit of unrighteous judgment, are those who are not standing on true anointing, but on a platform of influence gained by other means. Some received their position because of professional training, which came from schools founded upon a humanistic philosophy of journalism. This philosophy does have the appearance of wisdom and the search for truth, but actually is in conflict with the Truth Himself. Others may have been given a true commission from God, but have given way to the spirit of the world.

John said, "the whole world lies in the power of the evil one" (I John 5:19). The ways of the world are not the ways of God and, as Paul exhorted the Ephesians:

> **In reference to your former manner of life, you lay aside the old self, which is being corrupted in accordance with the lusts of deceit,**
>
> **and that you be renewed in the spirit of your mind,**

and put on the new self, which in the likeness of God has been created in righteousness and holiness of the truth (Ephesians 4:22-24).

If we are going to be **"created in right-eousness and holiness of the truth,"** we must put on a new self, and live by a different philosophy than that of the world.

Good Intentions

Many Christian journalists entered the field with the intention of trying to provide an alternative source of information to the secular media. This is a noble vision and is truly needed. The church is called to be the pillar and supporter of the truth. However, the accuracy level of reporting in Christian journalism has not proven to be any higher than in secular journalism—it only has a more "spiritual" slant to it.

The investigative reporting done by Christian journalists on the events that I have personally witnessed, or about people that I know, has been shockingly dishonest and untrue. Some were so prone to the use of gossip, hearsay, or even apparent imagination that they could rival some of the grocery counter tabloids. Truth is our most precious commodity, and we cannot continue to allow it to be compromised or we will receive the judgment that is promised for such deception.

Those who have been influenced by the humanistic philosophy of journalism may think we are shallow, blind, or duped if we do not expose the wrongs of others when we write about them. Yet it is much better to be ridiculed by men than it is for God to think of us as stumbling blocks.

The world's methods for seeking truth are very different from the way that real truth is found. Truth is only found in Jesus and can only be found when we are being led by the Holy Spirit. Secular schools may be able to teach us something about the mechanics of writing or the technical knowledge needed to understand today's media tools, but the philosophy that they sow into their students has been devastating when incorporated into Christian media.

Judgment on Journalism

Christian television ministries have come under severe judgment in the last few years. Television had given some people vastly more influence in the church than God had ever intended them to have. Whenever we move beyond the sphere of authority that has been appointed to us by God, we have moved beyond grace and we are bound to fall.

Other forms of Christian media are about to experience the same scrutiny that the television ministries have undergone. The Lord will ultimately deal with the secular media as well, but, **"it is time for judgment to begin with the household of God" (I Peter 4:17).** Christian journalism will soon come under the same kind of judgment that television ministries have been experiencing.

For a period of time, the public's trust and esteem of televangelists probably sank lower than that of any other professional group, including politicians and lawyers. There are, of course, politicians and lawyers who live their lives by the highest standards of integrity, yet they still must bear the judgment of their profession. This is because there are fundamental roots in these professions that must be corrected. There are likewise many journalists who sincerely attempt to live by the highest standards of truth and integrity, but they are often trying to do so on a foundation that simply will not support the truth. That is why the very foundations are being shaken, so that only that which cannot be shaken will remain (see Hebrews 12:25-28).

We will soon enter a period when Christian magazines, journals, newsletters, and newspapers will all come under the most intense pressure and scrutiny. The exposers are about to be exposed, and they will receive the same measure of judgment which they measured out to others. Even those who have tried to be honest and fair, but have been operating on a humanistic foundation, will see their faulty foundations collapse.

Can this judgment be avoided? The Scriptures clearly teach that judgment can be avoided by genuine repentance. As Paul told the Corinthians, **"if we judged ourselves rightly, we should not be judged" (I Corinthians 11:31).** Repentance is more than requesting forgiveness for our wrongs—repentance is going back to where we missed the turn and getting back on the right road. It also often includes restitution for the wrongs that have caused injury to others.

We must remember that the harvest is the reaping of what has been sown, and, **"in the way you judge, you will be judged; and by your standard of measure, it will be measured to you" (Matthew 7:2).** If we have sown unrighteous judgments, then judgment will soon come upon us. If we want to reap grace, however, we should use every opportunity that we can to sow grace. If we are going to reap mercy, we must use every opportunity to sow mercy. **"Do not be deceived, God is not mocked; for whatever a** man sows, this he will also reap" (Galatians 6:7).

The Grace of True Authority

According to the many examples in the New Testament, there are times when the errors of certain movements or sects must be addressed. The Lord Himself warned His disciples, saying, **"beware of the leaven of the Pharisees..." (Matthew 16:6).** Major portions of Galatians and other apostolic letters were devoted to correcting mistakes in doctrine or practice. The main difference between these Scriptural examples and what so often is done today is that the biblical writers had the *authority* to bring the needed correction.

Much of the reason for so much wrong judgment, or needed correction that is given in the wrong spirit or manner, is the vacuum that exists because those who truly have been given authority by God have refrained from using it. This does not justify the wrong use of authority, or the presumption of those who try to bring correction to the church without having the authority, but it does make such actions more understandable.

We can even appreciate the courage that some have had in addressing issues that no one else would address, but that still does not make it right. Even worse, it puts those courageous people in jeopardy of becoming stumbling blocks. Paul's lament to the Corinthians still applies to the church today:

> **Do you not know that the saints will judge the world? And if the world is judged by you, are you not competent to constitute the smallest law courts?**
> **Do you not know that we shall judge angels? How much more, matters of this life? (I Corinthians 6:2-3).**

Possibly the main reason that the church is so full of unrighteous judgment is because there is no format for *righteous* judgment in the church. Until the elders take their proper places in the gates, churches will continue to be subject to the judgment of the secular media and heresy hunters who, regardless of how well-intentioned they may be, sow division and unrighteous judgment which wound the body of Christ more than the errors they seek to expose.

The Lord has given mandates to the church that we cannot accomplish without unity. Righteous judgment is one of them. This issue must be addressed by church leaders on every level if we are going to accomplish our mandate for this hour. Unrighteous judgment is a source of most of the conflicts in the world. Since the church is called to be the light of this world, we should have the answers to the world's problems. How can we help to bring righteous judgment to the world if we cannot even judge ourselves?

Because of the many excesses of the past, or the tendency of some to presume authority beyond their appointed jurisdiction, it is understandable why we tend to shy away from this difficult issue. However, our continued neglect of this basic mandate to provide righteous judgment will prove increasingly costly. Until we bring proper judgment to the church, and then through the church to our society, we will continue to be subject to the unrighteous judgment of the world.